MIDHURST - THEN & NOW

Vic & Barbara Mitchell

Other Sussex books from Middleton Press, at the same price—

Branch Line to Selsey
Branch Lines to Midhurst
Branch Lines to Horsham
South Coast Railways—
  Brighton to Worthing
  Worthing to Chichester (in preparation)

First published 1983
Cover design—Deborah Mitchell
ISBN 0 906520 05 3

Published by *Middleton Press*
Easebourne Lane
Midhurst, West Sussex.
GU29 9AZ

Printed & bound by *Biddles Ltd.,*
Guildford and Kings Lynn.

WALKABOUT

—

Of all the towns I've been to
  In counties East and West
To live in or to look at
  I like our Midhurst best.

South Pond, Spread Eagle, church—
  The view delights the eye:
Old houses climb the hill
  In quiet dignity.

Follow the river round
  From Wharf to old North Mill,
Past castle site and Cowdray—
  Look back, and gaze your fill.

Or go on up past West Street
  Into the little Square,
And Georgian-fronted houses
  Will smile you welcome there.

Knockhundred Row will take you
  Into our broad North Street,
Where downland glimpses beckon
  Your eyes and eager feet.

Explore the place and ramble
  Around and up and down,
There's much that will entrance you in
  This picturesque old town.

Alec Annand

This book is dedicated to the late Charles White, professional photographer in Midhurst from 1948 to 1978, who compiled and published a book in 1972, "19th and early 20th Century Midhurst in old photographs". Herein we have included a number of unpublished photographs from his collection together with some of his own more recent work, and are grateful to Mrs. White for allowing us to do this. Unfortunately, all his negatives prior to 1964 were accidentally destroyed but we are trying to make good this loss and would be glad of the opportunity of copying any prints in your possession or, indeed, any photographs of old Midhurst. His former premises in Rumbolds Hill are now used as a wool shop. *(C. White)*

INTRODUCTION

The basic street plan of Midhurst remains almost unaltered since the first map makers recorded it many centuries ago. The earliest habitation was on the highest land where the narrowest streets exist today. Later development was in much wider streets—North Street and Bepton Road for example.

Only a small number of changes have taken place in the buildings of the town centre, partly due to the fact that the bombs of the last war were few in number and that the pressures for change that have influenced other towns have not been present here. These pressures include industrialisation and the effects of direct railway communication with London.

We have not set out to produce a history of Midhurst or to produce just an album of old photographs. We have attempted to reveal the change (and sometimes lack of change) that has taken place within the parish during the photographic era, by including a proportion of modern views which enables readers to make direct comparison without leaving their armchairs. We have restricted this album to the old parish of Midhurst (although we have stepped over the boundary a little to include North Mill, Cowdray and the railway stations) as we hope to compile a companion volume—Midhurst & District, Then and Now. The loan of photographs of the surrounding villages would be greatly appreciated.

The population figures for the parish reveal how slow the growth of the town has been.

1831	1,340	1921	1,890
1871	1,465	1931	1,812
1881	1,615	1951	1,895
1891	1,674	1961	1,880
1901	1,650	1971	2,169
1911	1,894		

The 1931 figures are not indicative of a plague—merely that the census was taken during the school holidays. Figures are not available for 1941, due to the war, and the 1981 population is not shown, due to boundary changes.

Our gratitude must be recorded to all those mentioned in the captions who have loaned photographs for copying and to all those, too numerous to mention, who have provided information or read the manuscript prior to printing. We apologise in advance for any errors therein which can occur due to the effect of time on the memory or the conflict of records.

We hope our readers will enjoy the journey back in time which progresses from south to north through the town, starting at the railway stations where most visitors used to commence their visit.

INDEX

The Midhurst of 1879 was much the same size as it had been in the previous 100 years or more. Notable developments to the west of the town had included the erection of the National School for boys and girls opposite the Half Moon, near to a point knows as Beggars Corner, and the building of several large houses in the country by the gentry. These included Sandrock, Guillards Oak, Ashfield House and Heathfield. Developments to the south included the erection of the Ebeneezer Chapel (now a sale room) and the Baptist Chapel (later the Masonic Hall). Further south the first railway stations were built. To the west of the Bepton Road can be seen the first station, which was that of the London and South Western Railway branch from Petersfield, opened in 1864. On the extreme left of the map can be seen the company's engine shed and turntable. To the east of the Bepton Road is the first station of the London, Brighton and South Coast Railway, which was opened in 1866, and was connected to the rival company's station by a footbridge. At this time the line from Chichester had not been built, neither had New Road. To the east of the town the gasworks is shown and, immediately to the right of it, careful examination will reveal the extent of the canal basin. Northwards, the location of the vicarage is indicated—-presently this building is occupied by the 'Crusty Loaf' cafe. Further north, the empty fields surrounding 'Dawsley Lane' (the road to Haslemere) can be seen. It was to be a further two to three years before the Victorian development of this part of Easebourne occurred. Scale 6 inches to 1 mile.

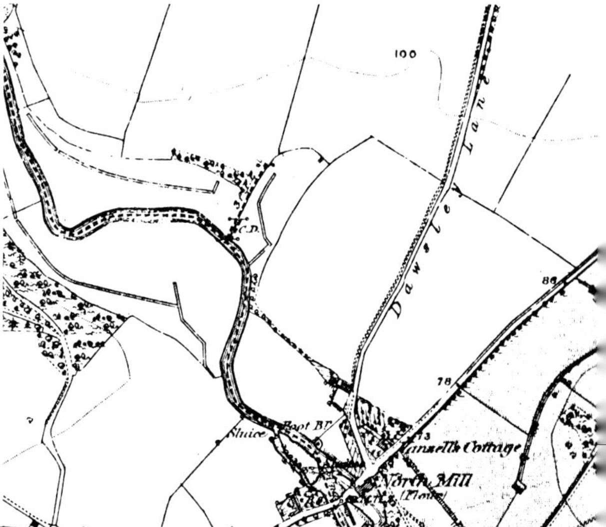

The 1897 map on the scale of 25 inches to 1 mile shows the vicarage to be on the opposite side of the street, opposite the Angel Hotel, and the Post Office to be at the south end of North Street, it later moving across the road into the building now used by the Co-op. Apart from the absence of Grange Road, the street plan is much the same as it is today. Note the boat-house at South Pond.

SOUTH OF THE TOWN

1. This postcard, postmarked 1909, shows the LSWR terminus at Midhurst which was the end of the branch line from Petersfield. The rails in the foreground allowed goods wagons to be transferred to the other station but, as the bridge over the Bepton Road was weak, they had to be hauled across by a horse, or a locomotive was sometimes used to give the wagons a push so that they would roll across the bridge by their own momentum. *(R. Carpenter coll.)*

Established 1854.

FARLEY & SON,
Coal and Corn Merchants,
Station Road, Midhurst.

ARTHUR WALLER,
Practical Tailor,
STATION ROAD, MIDHURST.

Liveries in all shades.

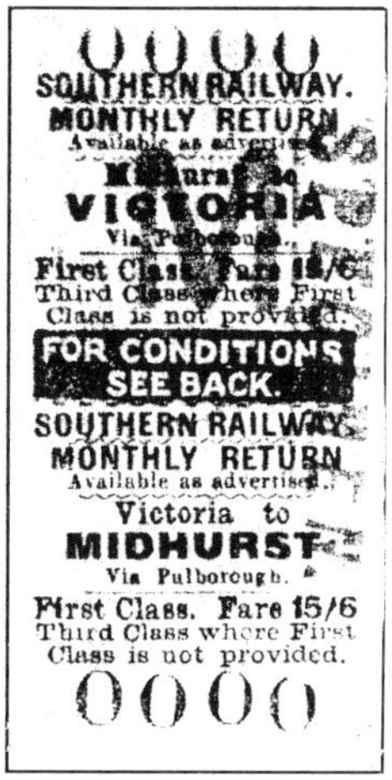

3. When trains ceased to call, the building was used, for about 40 years, as a dwelling, after which it fell into disrepair. Eventually, it was converted into offices, the classical Victorian windows being unexpectedly replaced by a Georgian style. *(V. Mitchell)*

2. The exterior view of the LSWR terminus shows the station master's five-bedroomed house with the single storey booking office attached. The station was closed in 1925, two years after the Southern Railway had incorporated the former rival companies and strengthened the Bepton Road bridge to allow passenger trains from Petersfield into the other station. *(Late E. Wallis)*

4. The Marshall steamroller was bought new by Midhburst Rural District Council in 1925 and is seen here leaving the WSCC Bepton Road Depot for the last time, on the 16th April 1983, prior to its presentation on permanent loan to the Chalk Pits Museum at Amberley. It may be seen there on public view between April and October (except on Mondays and Tuesdays). Behind the steamroller can be seen the former LSWR cottages, and the lanes on either side of this picture were the station approach roads shown on the first map in this book. *(V. Mitchell)*

B. R. HOWARD,

HAIRDRESSER, PERFUMER AND TOBACCONIST,

Station Rd., Midhurst

Private Saloon, with all the latest appliances, for Ladies.

FAMILIES AND SCHOOLS ATTENDED.

Razors Ground and Set.

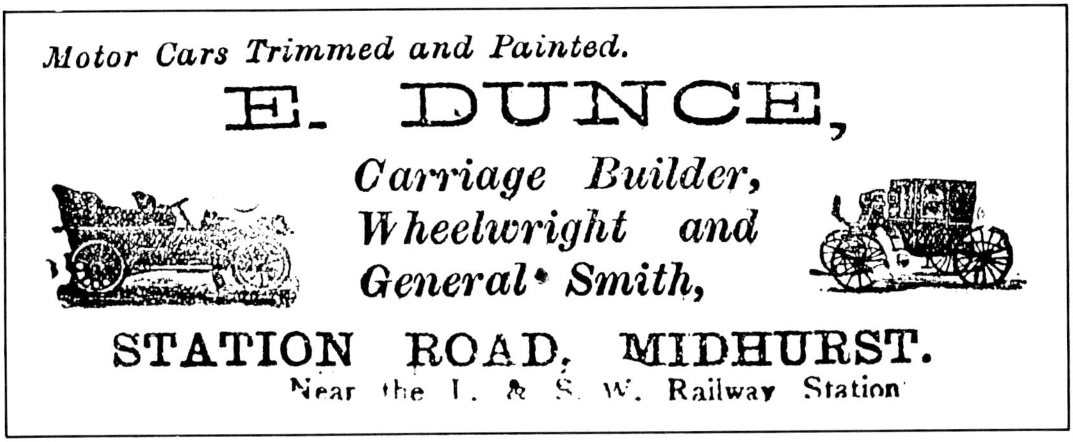

5. Victorian police stations were often built close to the railway stations as villains more commonly arrived and departed from the town by train and their comings and goings could therefore be easily observed. This elegant structure on the corner of New Road and Bepton Road (formerly known as Station Road) was demolished in 1974. Although elegant, its flint walls lacked the insulating benefits of a cavity, and its slate roof can be seen to be totally uninsulated. Another point of interest is that at that time it was located on a B road before the A286 was rerouted from South Street. *(C. White)*

6. When the London Brighton and South Coast Railway opened its line from Chichester to Midhurst in 1881 it had to build a new station further eastwards. The former station site was retained as a goods yard and the goods shed remains unto this day, in West's Timber Yard. This view of the new station was taken from the main signal box windows in 1925, the year in which Petersfield branch trains started running from the bay platform in the foreground. *(Late E. Wallis)*

7. Today the site is occupied by the Fire Station, Bourne Way and part of the Fairway. The tower is for drying fire hoses. *(V. Mitchell)*

8. This view was taken not long before the line was closed to passengers in 1955 and shows (from left to right) the cattle dock which was a scene of great activity in the polo season with the arrival of many horse boxes by train; one of the Aldershot & District Dennis Lancet buses which used to terminate at the station every thirty minutes throughout the day (although in the summei every fourth journey continued to Bognor Regis); the highly ornate Victorian station buildings; the typical one coach push-pull steam train and, on the extreme right, the little used but extensive down platform shelter. The full story of the railways to this town is told in 'Branch Lines to Midhurst' (Middleton Press). *(Lens of Sutton)*

E. & R. GATES,

DRESSMAKERS,

Chapel Mount, Station Road,

MIDHURST.

All Orders receive prompt and careful attention.

MODERATE CHARGES.

C. SPRING,

STATION ROAD, MIDHURST.

AGENT TO

ROYAL EXCHANGE ASSURANCE CORPORATION,

AND

ACCIDENT INSURANCE COMPANY, Limited.

Actuary of Savings Bank, Market Place, Midhurst

Open every Saturday from 11 to 12.

9. Isidor Livingstone Stent (telephone—9) operated a coal business and in the 1930s needed nine lorries and four horses to supply the town, which then had a population of under 2,000. No doubt he supplied surrounding villages as well, but not beyond the next railway stations, where other merchants would be trading. He also owned railway wagons—three appear in this picture. *(P. Stent coll.)*

ESTABLISHED 1854.

FARLEY & SON,

COAL FACTORS AND MERCHANTS,

STATION ROAD, MIDHURST.

SACKS LET ON HIRE.

Coke, free from Sulphur 10s. per chaldron at depôt, or 12s. delivered within a radius of one mile.

STEPHEN MILLS,

BUILDER & CONTRACTOR,

Timber Merchant & General Ironmonger.

STATION ROAD, MIDHURST.

W. BARLOW,

Purveyor of Meat,

STATION ROAD, MIDHURST.

10. The telephone exchange was manually operated until 1968, with all subscribers having simple 1, 2 or 3 digit telephone numbers. To call the doctor you simply asked for "six". On duty, near the end of the switchboard's life above the present post office we see, left to right, Mrs. Jarratt, Mrs. Leaf, Miss R. Matthews, Mrs. Bradley, Miss M. Gisborne and Miss M. Lockyer. *(C. White)*

11. At the same time a new fully automatic exchange, with 4 digit numbers, was being equipped, at the rear of the post office. *(C. White)*

SOUTH STREET

12. Looking north at South Street from the embankment forming South Pond which had been created prior to the 16th century for pisciculture (fish farming). Subsequently this water powered South Mill; later it was probably used to supply additional water to the canal in times of drought and now it serves the tourist industry.

The boater-wearing couple, in deep discussion, are standing by the pump that would have been used by water carts needed for wetting the dusty roads. *(C. White coll.)*

SAMUEL PARRISH,

LINEN & WOOLLEN DRAPER,

HATTER, HOSIER, HABERDASHER

AND

UNDERTAKER,

MIDHURST.

Agent for Nichol's Paletot and other Garments.

Agent to the Royal Exchange Assurance Company.

13. A recent view shows that the timber framed former market hall has been brought into view by the demolition of buildings formerly sited where cars now park. Otherwise little has changed, except one window has been replaced. Was it removed by a tax dodger concerned about paying window tax? *(V. Mitchell)*

14. South Pond has repeatedly become overgrown and silted up. This view from early this century illustrates the problem but cannot convey the smell which is now fortunately just a legend. As late as the 1940s, flooding of Pitsham sewage works upstream did nothing to improve matters. *(C. White coll.)*

15. A recent picture shows that although the pond is nearly full of silt again, the trees now receive careful management, to maintain a balanced view of town and country at this popular location. *(V. Mitchell)*

16. This view is from a postcard published by Maides Stores of West Street and hand dated 24th June 1918. All the buildings on the left have been demolished except the one-time market hall, part of which can be seen above the lean-to structure and also in the next picture, as a timber framed jetty. *(David Rudwick coll.)*

17. A recent view shows the Spread Eagle to be little changed, apart from the exposure of another window. Notice the fine carved wooden corner bracket. The Swan is showing signs of another attack by a lorry, and in the distance is the former South Mill, which for many years produced whiting for cleaning, amongst other things, cloth and leather. *(V. Mitchell)*

H. DUNCAN,
LATE J. OTHEN,
SOUTH STREET, MIDHURST.

BUILDER & CONTRACTOR,
MONUMENTAL AND GENERAL MASON.

Gas, Hot Water, - -
- - and Sanitary Engineer.
INCANDESCENT GAS BURNERS
and Fittings supplied and fixed at lowest charges

Plumber, Painter, & Glazier.

DECORATOR AND PAPERHANGER,
Sign Writer and Gilder.

Electric and
General Bellhanger.

SHOP AND OFFICE FITTER.

CABINET MAKER AND UNDERTAKER.
Funerals completely furnished.

Experienced Workmen in all Branches for Alterations and Repairs of every Description.

ESTIMATES FREE.

All kinds of Building Materials supplied at Moderate Charges.

PROMPT ATTENTION GIVEN TO ALL ORDERS.

The Midhurst Town Band
Wishes to inform the Gentry of Midhurst and district, and Committees of Public Entertainments, that their services are available for all kinds of engagements. The best military music is reserved for *Garden Parties* and other *high class engagements*. School Treats attended on reasonable terms. *Apply*—A. F. PAGE, Bandmaster, South Street, Midhurst.

18. A postcard from the early thirties shows the facade of the Spread Eagle, which contains mediaeval and Tudor features, and the former market hall in use as an antique shop, a trade which has proliferated in recent years. The proprietors of the Spread Eagle have recently published a booklet detailing the history of their premises. *(R. Carpenter coll.)*

A. H. Gillham,
FISHMONGER, ICE MERCHANT,
BUTCHER, PORK BUTCHER,
POULTERER, GAME DEALER,
MIDHURST.

ALL KINDS OF FRESH FISH DAILY.

19. For comparison, a contemporary view shows that the market hall, conceived in 1540, has sprouted television aerials to give entertainment to visitors to the town who occupy the overspill bedrooms of the Spread Eagle now located therein. The lower part of the hotel probably dates from the mid-eighteenth century whilst the curious mark in the road is due to the 1980 gas main renewal. *(V. Mitchell)*

ANTIQUES
ANTIQUES

20. In its early years ''ye Markett house'' had no walls to the ground floor and served as a covered market place where all the important business and trade of the district was carried on. The upper floor was used for public meetings but in 1672 it was also used as a school, for 12 boys, the school master being paid £20 a year. A similar market hall (from Titchfield) has been re-erected in its original form at the nearby Weald & Downland Open Air Museum. *(C. White coll.)*

A. AYLING,

SILK MERCER,

LINEN & WOOLLEN DRAPER,

SHAWLS, SILKS, GLOVES, HOSE, LADIES' BONNETS AND MILLINERY,

FAMILY MOURNING, FUNERALS FURNISHED.

MIDHURST & PETERSFIELD

Petersfield House, Midhurst.

Home School for Girls and Little Boys.

THOROUGH EDUCATION

Combined with home comforts.

PUPILS PREPARED FOR LOCAL EXAMS.

Recent successes include

College of Preceptors, London College of Music, Trinity College (London).

Special Attention given to Kindergarten.

Highest References from parents of pupils

Fees for Boarders £5 per term.

Principal: MISS CHALLEN.

21. In brief—"The Spread dorm. today"— with evidence of early herring-bone brickwork and a 1765 rainwater head. It receives much lorry bashing of a destructive nature. *(V. Mitchell)*

THE WHARF

22. According to Kelly's Directory of 1890 "Midhurst was lighted with gas by a company formed in 1860." The gasworks was situated on The Wharf close to the canal, which could transport coal economically, but it was not long before the railways arrived, offering even cheaper coal transport, despite the need to haul it by road from the fairly remote stations. Nothing remains of this scene, except the houses on the skyline which are in the turning opposite the Spread Eagle. Notice the tar boiler in this 1912 view and the white building, which was a council store and became the fire station in 1955. *(C. White coll.)*

23. A glimpse of the site of the former canal basin today, from St. Ann's Hill. The building in the left foreground is thought to have been part of the canal warehouse and is now part of a small trading estate. *(V. Mitchell)*

24. The Wharf fire station was in use from 1955 until the present station was opened in New Road in 1971. The volunteer part-time crew in 1964 comprised: (top row) H.H. Ayliffe, A. Whiting, R.D.J. Boxall, W.R. Parry, W.C.D.F. Clue, G.H. Wright, L.G. Saunders, H.G. Karn; (lower row) D.F.G. Gamblen, W.J. Bishop, R.E.F. Hoskins, W. Whiting, C. Madgwick, A.E. Gilbard, J.L. Clark. *(C. White)*

The best place for quality of work and
MODERATE CHARGES in
Steam, Hot & Cold Water,
Gas, Sanitary, and
ELECTRICAL ENGINEERING,
Pump Work, Machinery,
And General Whitesmithing is
E. CARPENTER & SON,
Midhurst; & Liss, Hants.
For all kinds of BUILDING we are positively
UNEQUALLED.

25. Canal barges could travel from London, Portsmouth or even the Midlands to Midhurst during the first half of the last century. This bridge was the last one on their journey and was located between the River Rother (which had been canalised by the provision of eight locks) and the canal basin. In Edwardian times a boat-house stood here, for storage of pleasure craft. *(C. White coll.)*

26. Today, the area is unfortunately heavily overgrown, despite some clearance work in connection with the creation of the Queen's Path in the year of her Jubilee, 1977. The keystone of the elegant bridge still bears the figures 1794. *(V. Mitchell)*

27. We will not attempt to describe the insanitary conditions prevailing in small country towns like Midhurst before the advent of main drains, but the erection of this ornate building signalled a time of joyous relief from previous suffering by local residents. Sewage (although discreetly not mentioned on the postcard) was pumped to the sewage works at Pitsham, south of the town. *(F. Maides coll.)*

28. With the construction of a new works (now politely called a treatment plant) east of the town, at South Ambersham, new pumps were required and a contemporary building style used, which does not include a weathercock. *(V. Mitchell)*

CHURCH HILL

29. This battered picture was taken just after World War I when demolition had started, prior to the erection of the war memorial on the site. One of the shops had been occupied by Mr. Mat Burnett, a Raleigh cycle dealer, who after having a fire on his premises is reputed to have sat up all night in case of a recurrence. He became almost a hermit, trading only in the evenings. *(C. White coll.)*

30. A few years later the scene was transformed and remains little changed today, despite recent attempts to move the war memorial. *(R. Carpenter coll.)*

31. Looking south towards the Spread Eagle, this undated postcard shows a cyclist close to the former Red Lion Inn, after which this street was named, although it is called Church Street at this end. *(R. Carpenter coll.)*

32. The bracket for the Red Lion Inn sign projects forlornly to this day. Many of the older buildings in this view are believed to be timber framed and removal of the rendering could reveal many details of interest. In the left foreground is a reminder of one of the less attractive features of the "good old days". *(V. Mitchell)*

33. Lyndale School for young ladies. *(C. White coll.)*

W. AUSTIN,

COMMERCIAL SCHOOL,

CHURCH STREET, MIDHURST.

Established above 20 years.

W. A's desire and aim being principally in developing the mental faculties of his pupils and cultivating business habits,

TERMS MODERATE.

34. Few would disagree that modernisation has improved the appearance of this building. Although photographed in mid-summer, every window is closed, whereas in the previous view every window is open to precisely the same extent. *(V. Mitchell)*

35. On the left is the chemist's shop at which H.G. Wells obtained his first job. He was sacked shortly afterwards and immediately visited Mrs. Allin, wife of the ironmonger whose shop faces us in this view. She was able to arrange a post for him at the Grammar School as an assistant master. *(R. Carpenter coll.)*

36.The roof line remains unchanged and at least one traditional trade still exists in the street. A farrier attends to the needs of local horses at a forge, near to the end of the row of cars on the left. *(V. Mitchell)*

37. Kensett was a draper, milliner and supplier of boots who was succeeded by Morley. Sheep Lane (on the right) was earlier known as Beast Market and at one time as Hog Lane—perhaps less desirable addresses to have. *(C. White coll.)*

— GO TO —

Kensett's for Novelties

An Up-to-date Stock of the — Latest Ideas in

Sports Coats, Jumpers, Coat Frocks and Costumes . .

TO BE SEEN IN OUR SHOWROOMS.
SUPERIOR PRODUCTIONS without Fancy Prices

BOOT REPAIRS a Speciality.

ROBERT KENSETT,

MIDHURST — LISS — PETWORTH

38. Two of the three bombs of World War II which fell on Midhurst exploded near here. One did a little damage near the library, but the other destroyed a cottage in Sheep Lane and killed, amongst others, an evacuee. Garages now stand on the site. *(V. Mitchell)*

T. AUSTEN,
LADIES' & GENTLEMENS'
FASHIONABLE
BOOT & SHOE MAKER,
RED LION STREET,
MIDHURST

GEORGE APPS,
BRAZIER AND COPPERSMITH,
Tin, Iron and Zinc-Plate Worker, Gas Fitter, &c.
CHURCH STREET, MIDHURST.

KITCHEN GOODS RE-TINNED AND REPAIRED.
utlery Ground and Umbrellas and Parasols neatly Repaired.

ESTABLISHED 1814.
Family Boot and Shoe Establishment.
Ladies', Gentlemen's and Children's
BOOTS & SHOES
In great variety kept in stock and made to order.
Sole Agent for
"K" BOOTS AND SHOES.
THE NOTED "E" BOOTS AND SHOES
ALSO PNEUMATIC BOOTS.
SIMMONDS,
THE GREAT BOOT,
Church Street, Midhurst
SPECIAL ATTENTION to repairs.
Patent Anhydrous Leather, perfectly waterproo .

39. This much admired corner of Midhurst consisted of cottages and one sweet shop, in this early 20th century view. *(R. Carpenter coll.)*

40. Photographed in 1921, we can note a number of small changes in the position and style of the windows when the building was in use as the Working Mens Club and when the streets were still gaslit. *(WSCC Library Service)*

Frederick Allin,
Furnishing & General Ironmonger
Church Street, Midhurst.

Patronised by the Rt. Hon. The Earl of Egmont.
Established 1866.

HENRY CLARK,
Hairdresser & Perfumer
CHURCH ST., MIDHURST.

Ladies and Gentlemen waited upon at their Residences.
Schools attended on reasonable terms.

NOTICE OF REMOVAL.

W. RUDWICK'S
LIVERY STABLES
Have been transferred from North Street to
MORE CONVENIENT PREMISES
AT CHURCH HILL
Adjoining Mr. Allin's Ironmongery establishment

ORDERS RECEIVED AT
Rumbold's Hill, opposite the L. & C. Bank.

41. The building has been commendably well preserved by the County Council, who have recently provided an access ramp to the library for the less agile, a feature seldom considered by earlier architects. *(V. Mitchell)*

Church Hill, Midhurst.

MIDDLE-CLASS SCHOOL FOR GIRLS.

Little Boys received up to ten years of age.

BOARDERS TAKEN WEEKLY AND QUARTERLY.

Principal—Miss CHALLEN.

42. The club, formerly at South Mill, was apparently closed down following a breach of the licensing laws, namely selling alcohol to non-members, in fact, two police officers! *(R. Carpenter coll.)*

43. Students of early building structure will be well rewarded by a visit to the library, as will lovers of art and photography who can enjoy the frequent exhibitions held on the premises. *(V. Mitchell)*

MARKET SQUARE

44. The west porch and gallery were added to the church in 1881, about 40 years before this photograph was taken, when the trees were of modest size. *(R. Carpenter coll.)*

LADIES' SCHOOL,

Edinburgh House, MIDHURST.

Principal—MISS NEWMAN.

Thorough preparation for all Examinations, including London Matriculation, Oxford and Cambridge Locals, Royal Academy and Trinity College, Music. Highly certificated resident Governesses. Visiting Professors. The pupils receive every home comfort and individual care.

Excellent references from parents of present and past pupils.

46. The weathercock usually eludes photographers but in 1971 it came down for renovation and to be shot professionally. *(C. White)*

45. Little can be seen of the church today as, like many good people, the trees have become grossly overweight. The lych-gate is a memorial to a former vicar, the Revd. F. Tatchell, who was a remarkably charitable man, a writer and great traveller, who died in 1935. *(V. Mitchell)*

47. On 13th June 1906, King Edward VII officially opened the Sanatorium that had been built to the north of Midhurst. Market Square was decorated as the King would travel this way from the LBSCR station. The Town Hall was at this time partly used to house the horse-drawn fire engine (note the fireman in the doorway), although it accommodated the Quarter Sessions from 1681 to 1809 and the County Court for some time after 1848. The upper rooms are now used by the Parish Church. *(C White coll.)*

48. In 1908 Lieutenant-General Sir Robert Baden-Powell wrote 'Scouting for Boys', and boys, also girls wanting to be like their brothers, took up Scouting. It was not until 1910 that the Girl Guides Association was formed with Miss Agnes Baden-Powell, sister of the Founder, as President, and until this time the girls just tagged on as self-styled Girl Scouts forming themselves into small groups with a name of their own choosing. This picture shows the 'Merry Maids' seated on a cart in the Market Square outside the church. *(C. White coll.)*

49. The first National school for infants could accommodate 120 pupils, but by 1890 it was only attended by 65. These were transferred to the school by the Half Moon and the building became Granville College, a private and superior place of education for girls. *(R. Carpenter coll.)*

THOMAS HOLT,
TEA DEALER, GROCER,
AND
CHEESEMONGER,
IMPORTER OF IRISH PROVISIONS,
Dealer in Corn, Malt, Hops, Hay & Straw,
Families supplied on the most reasonable terms,
MARKET SQUARE.

50. At present the building is used as the Red Cross Hall and is situated in a quiet and little known corner of Midhurst, off the Market Square. The back of the Town Hall and the side of the Swan can be seen at the end of the street. *(V. Mitchell)*

51. The earliest settlement in the area took place on St. Ann's Hill, a natural strong point, and included a massive house (the position of the thick walls can be seen today), a chapel (dedicated to St. Ann) and, underground, an ice house. The latter was surveyed fully in 1968 and here we see the entrance being measured. *(C. White)*

MRS. EDWARDS,
The Square, MIDHURST.
Apartments Furnished.

52. In mediaeval times and later, many large country dwellings had ice houses which consisted of deep stone or brick lined pits which were filled with blocks of ice, brought from nearby ponds or rivers during the extreme winters of those days. This gave a supply of ice throughout the following summer. *(C. White)*

53. A postcard by Burchnall, a familiar name in the town until recent times, of West Street viewed from the Town Hall. Note the ornate gas lamp brackets, the baker's delivery cart and the lady (with perambulator, as "prams" were then called) looking into what was formerly a fishmonger's window. *(R. Carpenter coll.)*

54. The market square has been resurfaced with granite setts and oak posts erected to prevent parked cars obstructing the view of our heritage. Unfortunately, the newly planted trees are beginning to do just that! *(V. Mitchell)*

WEST STREET

55. During the 70 years that have passed since this 1913 view was taken, little change has taken place in the buildings of West Street and many still house the same trades—on the left, greengrocer, watchmaker and jeweller, harness and saddle maker; on the right, a cycle shop and the Bricklayer's Arms. Notice that the cycle shop and Maides store sold petrol over the counter! At the end of the street we see the Congregational Temple. *(WSCC Library Service)*

56. Maides shop will be best remembered as a paradise for children, since it was, for many years, an extremely well stocked toy shop. In the late 1940s queues formed in early November for fireworks, then restricted to one 2/6d box each. *(M. Maides coll.)*

J. M. & L. MANSFIELD,
Leather Cutters, Glove & Gaiter Makers,
WEST STREET, MIDHURST.

Established 40 Years.

M. TODMAN,
WEST STREET, MIDHURST,
HAS NOW
WELL-APPOINTED BRAKES
For Parties; also
Landaus, Victorias, Pony Phætons and Dog Carts
For hire by the Day, Job, or Month.

57. Richard Green Ltd. incorporated Maides toy and stationery business into their adjacent hardware shop to form the present extensive shop. The doorway beyond the shop still leads to a water pump which predates mains supply. The skeleton at the end of the street remained inexplicably incomplete for over a year. *(V. Mitchell)*

58. In Edwardian days, before the days of the safety razor, businessmen of the town are recounted as having grouped outside this shop in the early morning to await their shave. *(C. White coll.)*

JOHN MORRIS,
TAILOR & WOOLLEN DRAPER
WEST STREET, MIDHURST.

Tailoring in every branch done on **the Premises,**
LIVERIES AS IN LONDON
Mourning Orders promptly attended to.

Established 1861.

G. HOLDEN,
Boot and Shoe Maker,
Leather & Grindery Seller.
WEST STREET, MIDHURST.

First-class Ready-made Goods only stocked.
Boots and Shoes made to measure by hand or machine at popular prices.
Repairing in all its branches executed on the premises, quick and cheap.
Brown Leather Dressings, Kid Revivers, &c.

59. The present shop front with glazed tiles and frameless windows contrasts with the earlier styles used elsewhere. *(V. Mitchell)*

60. Mr. Joseph Charles Ketterer was of German origin and although he had been trading in West Street for over 10 years before the commencement of World War I, he received such abuse from residents when the war started, that he committed suicide. *(C. White coll.)*

61. The Bannister family ran the business for several decades until succeeded by the present proprietor. The doorway to St. Johns, partly showing on the right, is a link with an important part of Midhurst's history, well described in the Illustrated Historical Guide, available from local bookshops. *(J.E. Allnutt)*

62. The day in 1968 when the embarrassed driver of a tank transporter took the wrong turning. There had been an earlier incident with a tank on this corner when, in 1941, a Canadian tank attempting to enter West Street broke the curved window glass on the corner of the shop. It never has been replaced to its full height, as can be seen on the left. *(C. White)*

PETERSFIELD ROAD

63. On 4th June 1966, the round Britain Milk Race passed through the town but attracted few spectators. This area received the third group of German bombs during an air raid in March 1943. The Congregational Temple and some cottages were destroyed and the premises of T.H. Russell Ltd., then on the north side of the road, were damaged. After repairs, a car showroom (now the Convent school gymnasium) and car hire offices were opened on the site. Theophilus Henry Russell was for many years cartage contractor to the two railway companies and also operated a Reo and a Siddley-Deasey coach for excursions. *(C. White)*

Convent, Petersfield Road, Midhurst.

SELECT EVENING CLASS.

Terms for English and Needlework,
1s. per week.

Private Lessons in Book-keeping, Music, Singing, French and Illuminating.
Piano available for private practice.

Laundry Work in all its branches, including "La Blanchérie et la Repasserie la plus fine."
Terms moderate.

Apply to the REV. MOTHER.

64. Residential development in late Victorian days occurred here, between the Petersfield and Bepton Roads, and also on the Chichester Road. These elegant terraces in Ashfield Road were supplied with iron railings and gates which were removed during the last war and melted down for re-use in weapon manufacture. *(R. Carpenter coll.)*

65. The houses still display the warm red of local made bricks and have not been defaced with modern textures and colour washes prevalent elsewhere. The original planners could not foresee the parking problems that would result from their designs. *(V. Mitchell)*

66. This postcard, dated 1907, shows two roads at different levels past the Half Moon. On the right can be seen the National School, built in 1854, remote from the town centre, on common land. It was enlarged in 1897 to accommodate 250 pupils. *(R. Carpenter coll.)*

67. Today the Half Moon is very popular with motorists, making photography difficult during opening hours. The school has been transferred to Ashfield Road and the buildings converted into dwellings. *(V. Mitchell)*

68. The road from Midhurst to Sheet became a Turnpike Road later than most, in 1825. Tolls were collected at this cottage and were used for the upkeep of the highway. *(WSCC Library Service)*

69. The toll house is a residence today and has become relatively lower to the road as the latter has become progressively built up. *(V. Mitchell)*

RUMBOLDS HILL

70. This 1931 view shows buildings on the right that have changed little since that time. However, on the left, on the far corner, the Omnibus & Horses has been transformed into a sports shop and, on the near corner, the 1907 Congregational Temple has given way to motor showrooms which have been recently converted into shops. When the enemy bombed the Temple they probably did not know that it was a strategic target—- namely the meeting place of the Home Guard, better known today as Dad's Army. *(WSCC Library Service)*

JOHN POATE,

Engineer, Millwright, and General Smith,

RUMBOLD'S HILL, MIDHURST.

Agricultural and other machinery of every description repaired. Lawn mowers repaired and sharpened.

Stoves and Kitcheners repaired.

71. On the 17th November 1980, Rumbolds Hill was closed and the splendid Victorian dome was replaced. The road had not been closed for that reason but had already been impassable for several days to allow for the renewal of the gas mains, which were over a century old and in any case designed for low pressure town gas. *(M. Chevis)*

MARSH PLANT
ROAD
CLOSED
PLUMB
KEITH'S
JOHN H

72. The International Tea Co. was the first chain store to open a branch in the town, a phenomenon which local traders viewed with great dismay in the 1880s. The staff was photographed in 1912. *(C. White coll.)*

74. In a sense, still international. The Chinese Restaurant was the first non-native place of sustenance to open in the town. Duck Lane, the turning on the left of this picture, had been in Victorian times a disreputable area of the town in which people feared to walk on their own. *(V. Mitchell)*

73. The company continued trading in the same premises until taking over the supermarket in North Street. *(C. White)*

75. In this splendid 1898 photograph we see Mrs. Waller's china shop (later Mr. Clark's) into which a passing cow is reputed to have walked! Unlike the proverbial bull, it did no damage. At the end of Wool Lane we can see Mr. Standford's van outside his West Street shop, which is still a grocers.

→

76. Unfortunately, in recent years, the Wheatsheaf has lost its distinctive chimney stacks, and the former Catholic Church has lost its bell. This church was built in 1868 and "afforded sittings for 70 people".

The Wheatsheaf
Fine Horsham Ales

77. The thoughtfully designed auditorium of the present Catholic Church gives passing aviators the impression that a piece of divine cheese has been placed on the Earth. Above it we see the square arrangement of the houses of White City, a development seldom seen by visitors (or indeed many residents of the district). The relatively small car park is obvious with the new white-roofed telephone exchange to the right. The triangle in the top of this view is the roadway of the Grammar School (Lower School). *(C. White)*

78. Wool Cottages, Wool Lane, photographed in 1931 with a car parked outside Glazier's sweet shop in Rumbolds Hill. The benevolent Revd. Tatchell started a Girls Club in 1918 in the cottage nearest to the camera and bequeathed it to his secretary in 1934. *(WSCC Library Service)*

79. The jetties and patterned tile hanging are a source of attention by camera-clicking tourists. This view shows how little change there has been in over 50 years. *(V. Mitchell)*

W. H. WAY,

Jobmaster and Carrier,

MIDHURST.

Horses and Carriages of every description on hire at Co-operative Store Prices.

Agent to the L.B. & S.C. Railway Company.

Town Bus and Flys to meet all Trains on L.B. & S.C.R.

Telegraph, Way, Midhurst. ***Office, Rumbolds Hill.***

L. BOXALL,

Draper, Silk Mercer, Hosier, &c.

RUMBOLD'S HILL, MIDHURST.

Millinery, Mantle & Dressmaking in the latest styles

BY EXPERIENCED HANDS.

WEDDING & MOURNING ORDERS.

80. Earlier known as Rum Balls Hill, the buildings have changed only slightly, the Grecian Urns having disappeared from the roof line, for example. The New Inn became the Egmont Arms of today. *(M. Maides coll.)*

81. Southward views present problems to photographers in all ages! This early morning shot shows, on the extreme left, part of the former Catholic Church (now a wine bar) and, in the distance, the tower of the present Catholic Church. *(V. Mitchell)*

82. Mrs. Pellett stands in the doorway of her half of the shop in about 1925, whilst Bill Whiting stands outside Daniels cycle shop, where he started work at age 14 years, often having to mend punctures until 10pm. Over 50 years later Daniels and Whiting are still familiar names within 100 yards of this spot. The former supply cycles in West Street and the latter electrical goods in Rumbolds Hill. *(W. Whiting coll.)*

Established 1883.

T. PRODGERS,

Fishmonger and Ice Merchant,

Wool Lane & Rumbold's Hill, Midhurst.

83. Viewed through the archway of the Egmont Arms we see the present merchandise of the same shop. *(V. Mitchell)*

NORTH STREET

84. This fine 1921 photograph contains a number of details worthy of note. The first door on the left is to the printing works, where Roynon produced the Midhurst Times. The ornate Public Hall, with its spirelet, was by then in use as a "moving picture house", posters giving details of Fox News and other films. Barclays Bank has arrived on the scene. The Model T Ford is a Hackney Carriage. *(WSCC Library Service)*

85. An early postcard shows the building that preceded Barclays Bank, with apparently a large wheeled tricycle parked outside. The personal message had to be written on the picture, as only the address was allowed on the other side. Later, regulations were changed and half of the address side could then carry words. *(R. Carpenter coll.)*

HENRY PESCOD,
WHOLESALE & FAMILY GROCER,
Wine and Spirit Merchant,
CORN, MALT AND HOP FACTOR,
North Street and West Street,
MIDHURST.

87. We have seen evidence of petrol being sold over shop counters. The next step was to erect petrol pumps outside the shop and sell it over the pavement, as seen on the right of this picture. This has now been outlawed and these were the last pumps in the district to serve petrol in this way, ceasing in May 1980. The purpose of the 1973 photograph was to show the traffic jams created by the traffic light experiment in Rumbolds Hill. *(C. White)*

86. An early morning view of North Street in the 1930s with the horse drawn refuse cart in the foreground, a curious vehicle to feature on a postcard aimed at securing good sales, but of interest half a century later. *(R. Carpenter coll.)*

88. The Public Hall was opened on 15th February 1882 by a limited company but the clock was provided by public subscription. The reading rooms contained a lending library, which was also a commercial venture. Opinion was, and still is, divided as to the merits of the architecture. Some felt it was too flamboyant and massive in relation to its neighbours. Others regarded it as an elegant complement to Hendersons and a unique bold Victorian contribution to the varied features of North Street. No doubt the physically handicapped had their own thoughts about the stone steps. The fine house on the corner of Lamberts Lane was the home of Dr. Holman at the turn of the century. Photograph date—1898. *(WSCC Library Service)*

Midhurst Grammar School,

Founded 1679.

Chairman...The EARL of EGMONT. **Head Master**...Horace Byatt, M.A.

Assisted by an efficient staff of Resident and Visiting Masters.

In this School boys receive a thoroughly practical Commercial Education, and Boarders have every home comfort. Numerous Certificates are annually gained from the Science and Art Department and the College of Preceptors, as well as University, Civil Service, and Pharmaceutical successes.

Terms on application.

London and South - - -
- - Western Railway.

Programme of a Grand Concert

IN AID OF THE

WIDOWS' AND ORPHANS' FUND,

AND

Railway · Servants · Orphanage · Fund.

Belonging to the Employees of the above Company, to be given in

THE PUBLIC HALL, MIDHURST,

On Friday, February 26th, 1897.

The following Ladies and Gentlemen have kindly promised to assist:

MRS. DOUGLAS SCOTT, VIOLIN, MISS ELIZABETH REYNOLDS, PIANO,

MISS MINNIE HYEM, G.S.M., SOPRANO,

MASTER EDGAR FAVELL, SOPRANO, MR. FRED COZENS, HUMOROUS,

ALZANDO GLEE SINGERS,

MR. FREDERICK MOORE, ALTO. MR. CLIFFORD HUNNYBUN, TENOR,

MR. SEYMOUR KELLY, BASS, MR. GEORGE FIELDER, BARITONE,

MISS A. PACKHAM AND MR. MOORE, ACCOMPANISTS.

The Grand Piano kindly lent by Messrs. Godfrey & Co., Southsea.

A Train will run from Midhurst to Elsted, Rogate, and Petersfield after the Concert, about 10.30 p.m.

Doors open at 7.30. Concert to commence at 8. Carriages at 10.15.

89. The side wall of Parkland Motors recently received chalk-written graffiti—just one word—''obscenities''. This well educated wit deserves recognition; as Midhurst is now twinned with a French town, Lamberts Lane could be renamed ''Rue de Remarques'' and as there are only a small number of premises located there, little inconvenience would be generated. The timbered building on the left housed the doctor's surgeries until the Health Centre was completed in Lamberts Lane. *(V. Mitchell)*

In Memoriam Cards.

G. ROYNON

Keeps a Large Stock of

The Newest Designs

At Prices to Suit all Classes.

Call and Inspect Specimens.

NORTH STREET, MIDHURST.

ORION

Cinema MIDHURST Sussex
Telephone 381
Manager: W. N. GAY

Continuous Daily from approximately 4.45 p.m

Matinee Whit Monday 2.20
CHILDREN'S CINEMA CLUB
Every Saturday at 1.45 p.m.

Prices of Admission
2/- 2/9 3/3 3/9
Children under 14 Half Price
(Sunday excepted)

PROGRAMME FOR JUNE, 1960

The Management reserve the right to alter this programme without notice.

90. Men only. An excursion which was probably passing through the town rather than starting in it. The solid tyres gave little comfort but the Tilling-Stevens petrol-electric transmission eliminated the rough gearboxes and clutches of the day. *(A. Lambert coll.)*

91. The Graffham buses of Hants and Sussex Motor Services (predecessor to Southern Motorways) started outside Barclays Bank, after turning via Lamberts Lane. The ageing Bedford OB was photographed in July 1961, with only one headlamp! In its later years, the cinema was partly painted and fitted with illuminated signs in an attempt to give a modern image and combat the effects of television on trade. *(A. Lambert)*

92. In 1928 the Angel Hotel still displayed its magnificent bracketed lamp over its doorway to supplement the well spaced gas lamp posts. Opposite, is the creeper covered vicarage, then the home of the Revd. Tatchell. Note the early radio aerial on the right. *(WSCC Library Service)*

93. With the foliage removed, the former vicarage (now local government offices) displays its unusual mathematical tiling, between its bay windows. Designed to look like bricks, they reduced the weight on timber structures and, at one time, avoided a brick tax. *(V. Mitchell)*

ANGEL BREWERY,

Public Hall Wine Vaults.

JOHN PARKER,

Brewer, Wine and Spirit Merchant,
Proprietor.

John Bridgen, *Florist and Seedsman,* North Street, Midhurst.	Established 1826. DAGWELL, Baker and Confectioner, NORTH STREET, MIDHURST. Daily Deliveries in Town and Country.

94. The generous vicar made his garden open to the public. Spot the naked figure! *(A.E. Whale/Mrs. O. Rudwick coll.)*

Local Views!
Local Views!!
Local Views!!!

The LARGEST and most VARIED ASSORTMENT of the above, mounted and unmounted in the newest designs, now obtainable of

G. ROYNON,

(late GOODNER,)

NORTH STREET,
MIDHURST.

INSPECTION INVITED

A Good Permanent Address.

"THE MIDHURST BUREAU"

Letters received and forwarded anywhere.

Registry Office for Servants.

For particulars apply:

W. PARSONS,

(late Marshall).

NEWS AGENT AND STATIONER.

North Street, Midhurst.

ANGEL STEAM BREWERY, MIDHURST.

JOHN PARKER, Proprietor.

ALES AND STOUT

Supplied in Casks of 4½, 9, 18, and 36 Gallons.

			s.	d.	
Mild Beer	X ..	at 9d. &	0	10	per gall.
Ditto	XX ..	at	1	0	,,
Bitter Beer	BB ..	at	1	0	,,
Mild Ale	XXX	at 1s. 3d. to	1	6	,,

			s.	d.	
Pale Ale	P A ..	.. at	1	2	per gall.
Superior Bitter Ale	B A	at	1	6	,,
Strong Ale	S A	.. at	2	0	,,
Stout	D S ..	.. at	1	6	,,

BOTTLED ALES.

	Per doz. Imp. Pts. s.	d.	
Parker's Dinner Ale ..	2	6	Patent screw stopper bottles.
Parker's Nourishing Stout ..	2	6	

	Per doz. Qts. s.	d.	Pts. s.	d.
Norfolk Cider	8	0 ..	4	6

Bass's Pale Ale, Guinness's Stout — Quarts, Pints and Imperial Pints.

German, Brighton, Schwepp's and other Mineral Waters.

SUPERIOR MALT AND HOPS.

Good Dinner Sherry at 24s. per dozen. Good Sound Port at 24s. per dozen. Max Gregor's Carlowitz. Wines of Superior and choice qualities. Irish & Scotch Whiskies. Parker's celebrated old Scotch blend. London Gin, Plymouth Original Ditto.

95. The same view today at least reveals the architectural details better. The principal bedroom is now the council chamber. *(V. Mitchell)*

96. A postcard franked 1910, shows the previous vicarage (by the lamp post) which the vicar converted into rooms for old people when he moved into the larger house that we have already seen in North Street. A room could be rented for 1d. a week and so it soon became known as the Penny House. On the left is "C.H. Newman, Farrier & General Smith", part of which later became the Southdown bus office. *(V. Mitchell coll.)*

"Is Life worth living?"
It depends upon the LIVER.

PODOPHYLLIN AND DANDELION PILLS.

Podophyllin is prepared from the dried root of the *Podophyllum Peltatum*, or American May Apple, and its action on the Liver is identical with that of the Mercurial preparations, but without their injurious effect on the constitution.

A Gentleman writes:—"Some little time since, I was troubled with Constipation and Indigestion; my liver was congested, stomach deranged, and appetite bad. A friend gave me a box of your Podophyllin Pills. I took one for two or three consecutive nights, then one twice a week for a fortnight or three weeks. I am glad to say my health has improved in every way, and I have lost the dull, morbid feeling I had, and experience a buoyancy to which I had long been a stranger."

DOSE.

Take one Pill every night until the bowels are acted on, then one at night occasionally.

Price 6d., 1s., and 2s. 6d. per Box. The 1s. and 2s. 6d. sizes sent by post for 12 and 30 Stamps.

These Pills are small & rendered Tasteless by being Silver-coated.

PREPARED BY

R. HUGGINS, Chemist,
199, STRAND, LONDON.

SOLD BY

G. D. WOLFERSTAN,
Chemist,
MIDHURST.

97. The farriers premises are now used by a building society and a greengrocer and the "Penny House" is now a cafe. *(V. Mitchell)*

D 6810

P
YBW 965R

98. Eventually, the bus office was moved over the road into the former "Penny House". A comfortable waiting room, with a fire in winter, was provided for passengers and parcels would be received for despatch to towns and villages anywhere on Southdown routes. Wine at 6/6 a bottle—32½p! Date—31st May 1959. *(A. Lambert)*

99. Mr. Charlie Tribe shoes a horse in 1908 at the rear of the premises that eventually became Midhurst Engineering & Motor Co. *(C. White coll.)*

100. A 1927 view, when horses were giving way to the horseless carriage. Notice the hand-cranked petrol pump and the AA petrol sign, fitted with cat's eyes in the lettering which no doubt reflected in the poorly focussed headlights of the day. *(C. White coll.)*

Pescod's Stores,

NORTH STREET, MIDHURST.

Telephone 15, ESTABLISHED OVER A CENTURY.

THE LEADING HOUSE FOR GROCERIES, PROVISIONS, &c.

Please Note.—This Establishment will Close Daily from 1.15 to 2.15 p.m.

J. Parker & Co's.,

BEERS AND STOUT

Have been Analysed, and Pronounced

Pure and Free from any Injurious Mixture.

APRIL, 1901.

101. The smithy at the rear had been transformed by 1928 into motor workshops. The large building, still visible down the narrow passage, was the Southdown bus garage for many years. *(C. White coll.)*

102. On the right of this 1933 picture is the well known Rosemary's Parlour, offering four course luncheons for 2/6 (12½p). On the extreme left we see the then relatively new electrical street lighting, whilst the post of its gas predecessor stands functionless opposite. By 1952 luncheon had been increased to 5/6 (27½p). *(WSCC Library Service)*

Rosemary's Parlour . Midhurst

Telephone 75 R.A.C. Main Road, near bus stop

Guest House

Old Walled Garden

Coffees, Luncheons & Teas

TARIFF

Terms (en pension)	*6½—8 guineas*
Per Day (Min. 3 Days)	*£1 1s.—£1 5s.*
Room and Breakfast	*17/6—£1*

Children - Reduced terms

Gas fire and ring in all bedrooms Interior sprung mattresses

Breakfast 3/6	9 a.m.
Luncheon 5/6	12.30 to 1.45 p.m.
Dinner 5/6	7 p.m.

W. G. GOSDEN,

Family Grocer,

WINE, SPIRIT, & BEER MERCHANT,

Maltster, and Hop Factor, Dealer in Hay, Corn Straw., and Meal,

NORTH STREET, MIDHURST,

Sole Agent in Midhurst and District for the Sale

OF

Royal Blend Whiskey as supplied to H.R.H. the Prince of Wales; Melrose Whiskey; The Anglo-Bavarian Brewery Company's Prize Medal Ales, in Cask and Bottles; and Fry &. Co's High-Class Aerated Waters, in Silvered Syphons.

103. A lull in the traffic at lunchtime. Rosemary's Parlour became offices for the Midhurst Rural District Council and after the demise of this authority the building reverted to residential use. *(V. Mitchell)*

104. To enable a bus stand to be created, these ornate gates and gate posts were removed piece by piece and re-erected at the far end of the causeway, closer to Cowdray Ruins. *(C. White)*

105. The causeway to the Ruins, with the roof of the present Cowdray House just visible in the distance in the trees. The white road markings indicate the former position of the gates. Midhurst still welcomes visitors and shoppers by offering free car parking and a regular bus service, at least north and south. *(V. Mitchell)*

Mrs. H. WALTON,
REFRESHMENT ROOMS,
(The Cyclists' Rest),
NORTH STREET, MIDHURST.

CHOPS & STEAKS
provided on the shortest notice.
Good Beds.

Established 1874.

T. B. MALLAM,
FAMILY GROCER,
Butcher and Provision Merchant,
Dealer in English & Foreign Fruits,
NORTH STREET,
(Next to Public Hall),
MIDHURST.

106. In 1970 this Guy bus belonging to Southern Motorways escaped on its own one night and ran away with the cattle. When the car park was created and the road from North Mill was widened, a splendid panorama across the meadows became available to road users. A few small trees were planted to enhance the surroundings but they have now grown to deprive us of a fine vista. Clearance of undergrowth and lower branches could make an agreeable harmony. *(C. White)*

FOR PRINTING

Of Everv Description

GO TO

The "Times" Office, Midhurst.

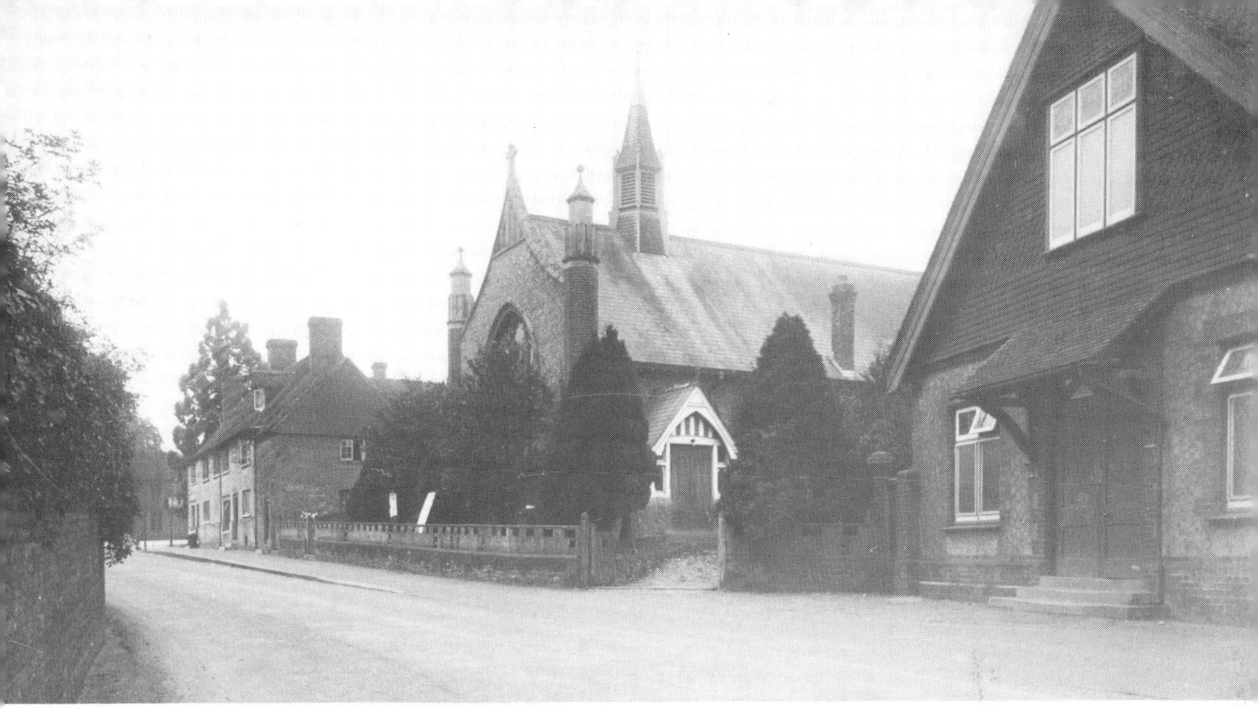

107. The Methodist Church, with spirelet, was opened on 25th May 1904, having been built at a cost of £2300. Behind the wall on the left a rifle range existed for many years. On the right is the Parish Church Room opened 7 years earlier. *(Mrs. O. Rudwick coll.)*

108. This church is now the only free church in the town and is attended by people of various denominations. The new lamp posts have been thoughtfully painted tree-trunk brown, unlike the stark concrete of nearby Easebourne. *(V. Mitchell)*

NORTH OF THE TOWN

109. Although Cowdray is over the river in Easebourne, no book on Midhurst would be complete without reference to it. The present house was constructed in stages following the disastrous fire of 1793 which left the previous house in the ruinous state that we are familiar with today. This 1913 view is little changed today, the main difference being the loss of the sun-room nearest the camera. *(WSCC Library Service)*

2, Vanzell Villas, Easebourne, Midhurst.

SCHOOL FOR YOUNG CHILDREN

(BOYS AND GIRLS)

English, French, Music, Drawing, Drill, Plain and Fancy Needlework.

The House is cheerful and airy, pleasantly situated, overlooking Cowdray Park.

The welfare of each Child is studied both as to health and happiness.

Prospectus on application to THE MISSES PEAT.

ARTHUR GILLHAM,
COAL AND COKE MERCHANT.

Oil, Petrol and Hardware Dealer, Jobmaster and Cartage Contractor.

Motor Cars for Hire.

'Phone 35, Midhurst.
EASEBOURNE, MIDHURST.

Easebourne Road, and Dodsley Lane,
MIDHURST.

STEVENS BROS.
FAMILY GROCERS,
WINE, SPIRIT, & BEER MERCHANTS

INSPECTION INVITED of our special stock of Carpets, Mats, China, Glass, Earthenware and Ironmongery at our DODSLEY LANE ESTABLISHMENT.

110. A variety of events have taken place in Cowdray Park over the years. In 1937 the 98th Surrey & Sussex Yeomanry, Queen Mary Field Brigade, Royal Artillery camped in the park. *(Mrs. G.A. Eames coll.)*

111. In the Christmas period of several years in the prosperous late 1960's, funds were forthcoming for the flood lighting of the Ruins. How impressive it was, especially as trees, which if well placed can be an asset, did not then obscure the view. *(C. White)*

JAMES STANFORD,
FAMILY BUTCHER,
Lutener Rd., Easebourne

All orders promptly attended to.

112. Even ruins need repairing! The first major conservation programme took place during World War I. This photograph was taken in 1969 of the only part still to have a roof. It houses the old kitchens and a museum. *(C. White)*

113. There had been a mill on this site as far back as the 12th century and was one of the most important possessions of the Lord of the Manor, at a time when Easebourne was of greater importance than Midhurst. For centuries it was powered by water wheels, but in its later years, turbines were employed. *(C. White coll.)*

FIRE

Insurance Society.

Mr. F. A. Tallant, Agent, Dodsley, Midhurst, paid TWELVE claims in this district during last year.

GWILLIM'S

Digestive SELF-RAISING FLOUR

BEST CHEAPEST AND GENUINE.

Forage and Provender

UNDER

Government Control.

NORTH MILL, MIDHURST,
COULTERSHAW MILL, PETWORTH.
WASSELL MILL. EBERNOE.

114. Tasteful conversion to residential use has enabled the general outline to be conserved and sensitive control of trees has retained views, inwards and outwards. The ventilator and finial on a modern garage is a touch of genius. *(V. Mitchell)*

115. The central character has his hand on the crown wheel, a gear fitted with apple wood teeth and attached to the upright shaft by means of wooden wedges. In the foreground are the mill stones and, in the background, there is their circular wooden cover. Woodworms and rats were the only occupants when this photograph was taken in 1969. *(C. White)*

H. DUNCAN,

LATE J. OTHEN,

BUILDER & CONTRACTOR,

Monumental & General Mason.

A. MILLS & SON,

Family Grocers and Provision Merchants,

Lutener Road, Easebourne.

THE "ROTHER" INN,

EASEBOURNE, MIDHURST.

116. At the same time we see the wheel shaft over the wheel pit, the wheel having been removed many years previously. The last millers were Bartholomews of Chichester. *(C. White)*

117. North Mill and Mill House, around 1930, showing a sack chute, to speed the loading of carts or lorries. Mains services ruined the appearance of the bridge which was later further disfigured by the addition of a cantilevered footbridge. *(A.E. Whale/ Mrs. O. Rudwick coll.)*

118. The value of the separate wooden-boarded footbridge is apparent in this view. A car has had to reverse onto the former footpath to allow the bus from Aldershot to creep past it. Oh for a bypass!

..... and as in the past, Midhurst is still the town where many folk from neighbouring villages meet together for education, healing, business, work and leisure. The caring spirit that exists here is perhaps epitomised by the carving of clasped hands to be found on North Mill bridge, the boundary between Midhurst and Easebourne; but we must leave the stories of the villages for another day.